Success with
Rock Gardens

ALMUTH SCHOLZ

Series Editor
LESLEY YOUNG

MEREHURST

Introduction

Contents

An enchanting corner

What could be more harmonious or in tune with nature than flowers basking in the sunlight in all colours of the rainbow, decorative seedheads and rocks and stones attractively arranged in a well-planned rockery.
In this guide, rockery expert Almuth Scholz explains how to create the perfect rockery and how to ensure that it will boast a wealth of flowers almost all year round.
You will find ideas on designing for both sunny and shady spots, for a miniature rockery or for a nook beside water. The carefully designed, easily followed planting plans contained in this guide have been developed by the author after years of practical experience. Use them to simplify the task of planning a rockery that is made to measure for your own garden. There are also practical pages filled with detailed information on topics such as the botany of alpine and rockery plants, choosing rocks and stones and on building a drystone wall. Stunning colour photographs invite you to browse through a tempting selection of plants that are suitable for all situations.

Phlox, pinks and yarrow in glowing colours.

Campanula.

Rock rose.

The author

Almuth Scholz is a self-taught gardener who has been a passionate advocate of "natural" plant communities all her life. To this end she designs gardens, runs seminars and provides advice from an environmentally friendly standpoint. In her work the author places great emphasis on designing plant communities that are close to nature in individual areas of the garden and on combining suitable woody species and trees.

The illustrator

Marlene Gemke studied graphic design at the Fachhochschule Wiesbaden and now works in a freelance capacity as a scientific illustrator. She has been an illustrator of animal and plant subjects for many years and has produced several of the illustrations in the "Success with ... " series.

NB: Please read the Author's Notes on page 61 in order that your enjoyment of alpine and rockery plants will not be impaired.

Your rockery

A rockery that has been designed to resemble nature as closely as possible is like a piece of a beautiful landscape that has been dropped right into your own garden. Rockeries are usually fairly undemanding so it is quite easy to provide the right conditions. After even a short time you will find that nature is beginning to colonize your rockery.

Above: The glowing yellow flowers of the evening primrose.
Left: Water can form an attractive design element in a rockery.

Your rockery

Attractive at any time of year

A rockery will provide an eye-catching feature all year round with a wealth of colourful flowers, interesting leaves and attractive fruit and seedheads. If you grow scented plants, it will be a delight to your sense of smell as well as a visual pleasure for your eyes. It can also form a small portion of a "designed" natural habitat within your own garden.

Natural-looking garden design

Designing a rockery offers many possibilities for expressing an ecological approach to gardening. You will be able to create suitable habitats for many creatures within rockeries and drystone walls, while still designing them to look natural and be functional.
Even natural gardens have to be consciously designed by humans. Paths should not be allowed to become overgrown, beds should not suffocate in weeds, although both design and care must remain in harmony with nature.
Several points should be considered when planning your natural garden.
Observe and incorporate existing natural conditions: The existing natural conditions are the soil, water supply, light,
climate and the natural environment.
● The consistency and structure of the soil should be of particular interest to you. You may have a sandy, loamy or clay-rich soil, nutrient-poor or nutrient-rich (see p. 22).
● The water supply will be closely connected with the structure of the soil. Sandy soils are scarcely able to store water; soils rich in clay have a great capacity to absorb water. However, the level of precipitation in your region will also play a part.
● Conditions of light are also important for the type of design and the choice of plants.
● The climate – there is an important distinction between the macro-climate and mini-climate – will greatly influence growing conditions in your garden. The macro-climate is the general climate of a whole region or area. The mini-climate refers more to the particular climate in your garden or even a corner of it. Have you got hedges, for example, that will provide windbreaks, or large trees that will absorb much water and reduce light?
● You should not forget the natural environment around your garden. A garden in a wood must be designed differently to one on a sunny slope.
The use of plants and materials that are suited to the locality: If you take the natural
conditions into consideration, you will be able to choose plants that will feel quite at home in your garden (see pp. 14/15 and 18/19).
The design materials I use are mainly rocks and stones. If possible, use rocks and stones that are complementary to your locality and type of soil. For chalky soils, choose limestone of various kinds and shapes. Granite, basalt or sandstone will go well with lime-poor soils that support acid-loving types of plants. Unwanted rocks and stones obtained from the landscape around your own garden are very suitable for small rockeries. (Do obtain permission before you take what may seem to be "unwanted" stones!)
Copying natural environments: You will be able to create a rockery biotope with appropriate plants and materials. Within a few years the plants and rocks will form a distinct and integrated biological niche in which many creatures will find shelter and nourishment. You will not need to provide much care in such a naturally evolved installation (see p. 48).

Protecting the natural environment

Do not use any plants taken from the wild. Most wild plants are protected by law and, anyway, would not thrive if taken from

Gentian and edelweiss turn their flowers towards the sun.

their natural habitat. All good nurseries will have a wide selection of well-grown rockery and alpine plants.

The origins of rockery plants

The wild species of our rockery plants come from high mountain regions all over the world; for example, in Europe from the Alps, the Carpathian Mountains, the Pyrenees and the mountains of Scandinavia; from the Himalayas in Asia and from the Rocky Mountains in America. Hot steppe landscapes are another type of region from which these plants originate. Similar extreme conditions prevail there as in mountainous regions. Such special conditions of growth include intense light from the sun and a high proportion of UV rays, extreme fluctuations of moisture, great differences between day and night-time temperatures, a large amount of snow in winter, a short vegetation period, a thin layer of humus, constant air movement and the capacity of rocks and stones to store heat and water.

Botany

The botany of rockery garden plants is determined by the extreme conditions to which they are often subjected in their natural environments.

Rockery plants are mainly herbaceous plants

Rockery plants are robust, perennial plants. They have adapted to a particular form of overwintering – through overwintering buds. These are situated in storage organs that are either subterranean or close to the ground and from which new shoots emerge every spring.

Shapes of growth
(illustrations 1-5)

Rockery plants tend to live in close proximity on rocks and stones. Although there are many transitional types among them I have divided them up into four groups, based on their shapes of growth. Cushion rockery plants grow into very large cushion-like clumps over the years and may trail down rocks or

slopes (see illustration 1). Many evergreen species, like rockery phlox or alyssum, belong among this group of plants. Their long tap roots enable them to dig in between large rocks or stones; they can grow into narrow cracks and are able to obtain nourishment from deeper layers of the soil.

If they are able to make contact with the soil – for example, if you lay stones on top of them – their shoots will form new roots and produce new plants in the process.

Mat-like rockery plants (see illustration 3) form runners or rhizomes that grow roots and thereby form regular carpets of plants. They, too, will cover rocks, stones and parts of walls and will only continue to grow outwards if they can find a suitable foothold. Among this group, for example, you will find species of thyme that form mats. A special form of such groundcover plants are rosette-forming plants (see illustration 2).

2 Rosettes are most attractive plants.

These produce decorative leaf rosettes that lie on top of the soil. Short runners grow out in all directions to form new rosettes. Small stonecrop species and many saxifrage types are included among these plants.

Bushy species (see illustration 4) form compact, small plants with quite large rootstocks. They look better in rockeries if they are planted in small groups. Edelweiss and pasque flower belong among this group of plants.

Like the cushion plants, they produce rather long, large rootstocks that reach deep down under the stones and rocks. While the above-

1 Cushion plants root in one place and spread out over a large area.

3 Mat-forming rockery plants produce rhizomes that will root in a new position.

ground parts profit from the warmth stored by rocks and stones, the roots are protected in the cool soil underneath them.

Sub-shrubs (see illustration 5) form a transition to the dwarf shrubs. Some of them produce woody branches near the base of their roots. They can be encouraged to form compact, bushy growth through vigorous cutting back. In mountainous regions they are kept naturally low and small through the action of constant wind and thick layers of snow. Lavender or rock roses are sub-shrubs of this type. They use their strong roots to cling to stony slopes and loose scree.

Flowering times and colours

The main flowering time for rockery plants is in the spring and early summer. The short vegetation period found in the mountains means that alpine plants come up out of the soil very fast in the spring. After long, colourless winter months, you will be overwhelmed by their fiery, glowing colours. The particularly intense colours are a result of the high intensity of light in the mountains. For this reason, it is a good idea to plant alpine plants in full sunlight. During the summer months the majority of rockery plants produce more delicate flowers in

pastel shades. Various different leaf colours, particularly when combined with feathery, ornamental grasses, look particularly good at this time.

Towards the autumn, highlights of colour are provided by carline thistle (*Carlina vulgaris*), pearly everlasting (*Anaphalis*) and heathers. Seedheads of some early-summer-flowering species provide attractive variation. You will be able to achieve special colour effects in larger plantings through the use of taller growing flowering rockery plants and some dwarf shrubs and trees – for example, species with bright autumn foliage and colourful fruits.

Leaf shapes and structures

Rockery plants are not only useful for their flowers, but also for their great variety of leaf shapes and structures. Silvery foliage, fleshy leaves, leaf rosettes, downy leaves in different colours or decorative leaf shapes will enhance the look of even the smallest rockery bed. In their natural habitats, these plants evolved such leaf shapes to protect themselves from lack of water and intense sunlight. Using such plants you can happily install a rockery facing due south without fearing that watering will become a tedious chore in the summer months.

4 Pasque flower is best grown in groups.

5 Lavender is a strongly scented sub-shrub.

A rockery biotope

Many attractive varieties of houseleek can be found.

This euphorbia provides shelter for a ladybird.

Rockery plants for many occasions

Rockery plants grow in the most varied conditions in their natural habitats in mountains or steppes and, depending on the species, they can be planted in very different positions in the garden:
● on chalky or lime-poor soils;
● in sunny or shady positions;
● in dry or marshy, moist positions.

The rockery plants found in garden centres are cultivated forms derived from the wild species of mountain and steppe plants.

After much crossing and work by plant growers, they have become more or less adapted to life in gardens, depending on the species in question. This means that many robust species are perfectly well suited to situations in gardens that are very different from conditions in their original habitats. The wide range of species and their variability have been greatly improved through artificial selection and crossing. Provided rockery plants are chosen according to their requirements with respect to position, they will feel right at home in your garden and will blend to form natural-looking, decorative plant communities. These mature plants will form dense carpets that can be further enhanced through the careful positioning of rocks and stones, and by planting grasses, ferns and larger bushy species. Interesting planting designs are possible for sunny, dry spots (see p. 36) but also for shady positions (see p. 40). Steps and paths are ideal as well as the rocky edges of small pools of water or streams (see p. 44). A rockery biotope that is copied from nature will still give you plenty of leeway for creative design.

Requirements common to all rockery garden plants

All rockery garden plants share three common characteristics.
● Rockery plants require soil that is water- and air-permeable. The waterlogging that may often be inevitable in clay-rich soils, particularly in winter, is detrimental to rockery plants. If soil conditions are not good, improved drainage will become vital (see p. 22). Heavy soils should also be improved with compost.
NB: You will be able to grow rockery plants that like alkaline soil as well as those that like acid soil in such well-aired soils.
● There are two groups of rockery plants – plants for dry positions with a lot of sun, and plants for shady positions with moist soil and high humidity. You will be able to combine these two groups of plants in large rockeries. Large rocks, artificially designed hollows and sunken

paths will provide shady spots that can be planted with varieties that like cool positions. Water in a rockery will provide high humidity. Beds edged with bushes or trees, or positioned under large trees, are less suitable for rockery plants as shade and dry conditions are combined here. Also, the soil here will be fairly well compacted by the tree roots. Only dwarf plants and trees that originate from mountain regions will provide suitable, decorative design elements for larger rockeries.
● Mountain plants "hibernate" through the winter under a thick layer of snow. The snow protects them from severe frosts, cold and wet, and from drying out under the winter sun. The snow layer is also light-permeable so the plants are able to prepare their new shoots under the snow. In temperate, low-lying regions, in which there is relatively little snow, rockery plants are particularly at risk from the effects of winter sunshine and cold, wet conditions. The provision of a drainage layer and loose soil will help plants to survive wet, cold winter conditions. Particularly sensitive plants can be protected from very severe frosts and winter sunshine by placing a loose layer of conifer brushwood on top of them (see winter protection, p. 52). The conifer needles will begin to drop off by the spring so

the plants will gradually get used to different light conditions and can prepare new growth.

Wildlife in a rockery

Once a suitable equilibrium has been established within a rockery biotope, many creatures will colonize it automatically.
This ecological equilibrium will be determined by the conditions of the position, and by the presence of suitable plants and rocks and stones. Rockeries, drystone walls and garden ponds can all develop into balanced biotopes that support wildlife. In larger installations, where wildlife is less disturbed, creatures such as slow worms or lizards may arrive, and frogs and toads will appear in damp hollows and beside pools of water. Birds that nest at ground level may also utilize cushion plants and niches between rocks or stones for nesting sites. Even small mammals such as shrews will find food and shelter in a rockery.

Carline thistle.

Bright cheerful colours in a sunny position

A rockery in a sunny position can appear like a brilliant jewel set in a larger garden complex. You can choose from pure white to brilliant yellow to countless shades of pink, violet and blue.

Thrift flowers produce a glowing pink splash of colour.

Evening primrose.

Crane's bill.

White campanula.

Blue campanula.

Pasque flower.

Many plants that are well suited to rockeries originate from natural habitats in high mountain regions where they are just that little bit closer to the sun than other plants down below. For this reason, they will be regular sun worshippers when they are grown in your own garden. They stretch out their flowers towards the light and also grow towards the source of light.

Whether they are pasque flowers in many different colours, campanula of several different types or even the elegant but prickly carline thistle – they are all quite obviously happy to bask in full sunlight.

A rockery biotope

Plants for sunny positions

Name	Position	Soil	Shapes of growth / Height in cm/in	Flowering time / Colour	Neighbouring plants	Comments
Achillea / yarrow	○	d	15-20 cm (6-8 in) / cushion	ES-LS / white, yellow	Lavandula, Nepeta / Veronica, grasses	heathland or steppe garden, low growing species and varieties
Alyssum / alyssum	○	d / l	15-30 cm (6-12 in) / cushion	LSP-ES / yellow	Arabis, Aubrieta, / Iberis, Phlox subulata	silvery foliage, walls, ground cover, evergreen
Anaphalis / pearly everlasting	○	d / l	20-40 cm (8-16 in) / bushy	MS-LS-MA / white	Alyssum, Linum, / Sedum telephium	silvery foliage, heathland garden
Antennaria / mountain everlasting	○	d / a	15 cm (6 in) / mats	ES-MS / white, pink	Dianthus deltoides, / Thymus, over bulbs	heathland garden, ground cover
Arabis caucasica / garden rock cress	○	d / l	15 cm (6 in) / cushion	MSP-LSP / white, pink	Alyssum, Cerastium, / Iris barbata-nana	walls, evergreen
Armeria / thrift (sea pink)	○	d	15 cm (6 in) / cushion	LSP-MS / pink, white	Potentilla / Iris barbata-nana	walls, evergreen
Aubrieta / aubrieta	○	d / l	10 cm (4 in) / cushion	MSP-LSP / blue, red	Alyssum, Iberis, Phlox / subulata, Iris barbata-nana	walls
Campanula / campanula	○–◐	d / l	10-20 cm (4-8 in) / cushion	LSP-LS-MA / white, blue	Alchemilla, Dianthus, / Geranium, Sedum	walls, low-growing species, partly evergreen
Carlina / carline thistle	○	d / l	5-30 cm (2-12 in) / bushy	MS-MA / white	Helianthemum, Linum, / Origanum, grasses	heathland garden, winter decoration
Cerastium / snow-in-summer	○	d	15 cm (6 in) / cushion	LSP-ES / white	Campanula, Linum	walls, silvery foliage
Centranthus / red valerian	○	d / l	60 cm (24 in) / hanging	ES-EA / red, white	Potentilla, Veronica	self-sowing
Dianthus / rockery pink	○	d / l	15 cm (6 in) / cushion	ES-LS / red, pink	Gypsophila, Thymus, / Potentilla	D. deltoides (hates lime!), heathland garden, evergreen
Dryas octopetala / mountain avens	○	d / l	10 cm (4 in) / mats	LSP-MS / white	Campanula, Gentiana, / Gypsophila, grasses	decorative fruit, evergreen, surface-covering
Eriophyllum lanatum	○	d / l	30 cm (12 in) / bushy	ES-LS / yellow	Lavandula, Nepeta, / Origanum, grasses	silvery foliage
Erinus alpinus / fairy foxglove	○	d / l	10 cm (4 in) / mats	LSP-LS / pink, white	Iberis, Saxifraga	self-sowing
Festuca	○–◐	d	20-30 cm (8-12 in) / bushy	ES-MS	Achillea, Carlina, / Dianthus, Inula	decorative in winter, evergreen
Gentiana / gentian	○–⊙	m / l	10-15 cm (4-6 in) / mats	LSP-MS-LS / blue	Alchemilla, Primula, / Leontopodium, Geum	partly evergreen
Geranium / rock geranium	○–◐	d / l	15 cm (6 in) / bushy	ES-EA / pink	Campanula, Silene, / Helianthemum	autumn colours, long-lasting flowering period
Gypsophila / baby's breath	○	d / l	15 cm (6 in) / cushion	LSP-LS / white, pink	Campanula, Linum, / Geranium	low-growing species, long-lasting flowering period
Helianthemum (hybrids) / rock rose	○	d / l	15-20 cm (6-8 in) / semi-bush	ES-LS / yellow, white	Geranium, Linum, / Carlina, grasses	cutting back encourages further flowering, evergreen
Heliosperma alpestre	○	d / l	15 cm (6 in) / bushy	ES-LS / white	Petrorhagia, Veronica, / over bulbs	

Plants for sunny positions

Name	Position	Soil	Shapes of growth Height in cm/in	Flowering time Colour	Neighbouring plants	Comments
Iberis perennial candytuft	○	d l	10-20 cm (4-8 in) cushion	ESP-MSP white	Alyssum, Aubrieta, Viola, tulips	walls, evergreen
Inula ensifolia "Compacta" fleabane	○ – ◑	d	20 cm (8 in) bushy	ES-EA yellow	Gentiana, Linum, Origanum, grasses	long-flowering
Iris barbata-nana rockery iris	○	d	25-30cm (10-12in) bushy	MSP-LSP mixed colours	Iberis, Phlox subulata, Pulsatilla, Aubrieta, grasses	
Koeleria glauca	○	d	40 cm (16 in) bushy	ES-MS	Geranium sanguineum, Linum, Pulsatilla	winter decoration, ground cover
Lavandula lavender	○	d l	40 cm (16 in) sub-shrub	MS-EA blue, pink	Eriophyllum, Sedum, Oenothera, Origanum	silvery foliage, scent, evergreen
Leontopodium alpinum edelweiss	○	m l	15 cm (6 in) bushy	ES-LS white	Gentiana, Saxifraga, Campanula	seedheads, silvery foliage
Linum flax	○	d	25-30cm (10-12in) bushy	LSP-MS blue, yellow	Achillea, Potentilla, grasses	wall
Nepeta fassenii cat mint	○	d l	30-50cm (12-20in) cushion	ES-EA lilac, blue	Achillea, Alyssum, Centranthus, Potentilla	heathland garden, cutting back encourages further flowering
Oenothera missouriensis evening primrose	○	d l	15 cm (6 in) bushy	MS-EA yellow	Cerastium, Nepeta, Lavandula, Sedum	remove seeds, long-flowering
Petrorhagia saxifraga	○	d l	20 cm (8 in) bushy	ES-EA pink	Campanula, Sedum, Heliosperma	wall
Phlox subulata moss phlox	○	d	10-15 cm (4-6 in) cushion	LSP-ES red, lilac, white	Iberis, Aubrieta, Veronica, Iris	wall, evergreen
Potentilla rock cinquefoil	○	d	5-40 cm (2-16 in) mat	LSP-LS yellow, white	Campanula, Linum, Pulsatilla, Thymus	ground cover
Pulsatilla vulgaris pasque flower	○	d	20 cm (8 in) bushy	MSP-LSP lilac, red, white	Carlina, Antennaria, Inula, Crocus, grasses	decorative fruit
Sedum stonecrop	○	d	5-40 cm (2-16 in) mat	MSP-EA yellow, white	Dianthus, Thymus, Potentilla, Anaphalis,	partly evergreen, wall
Sempervivum houseleek	○	d	10-20 cm (4-8 in) rosettes	ES-LS yellow, pink	Iris, Sedum, Saxifraga, grasses	evergreen, wall
Silene moss campion	○ – ◑	d l	5-20 cm (2-8 in) cushion	LSP-ES-MA white, pink	Leontopodium, Sedum, Geranium, Helianthemum	wall
Stipa	○	d l	20-40 cm (8-16 in) bushy	MS-LS	Carlina, Helianthemum Origanum	very decorative, low-growing species
Thymus thyme	○	d	5-20 cm (2-18 in) mat	LSP-EA pink, white	Carlina, Iris, Alyssum, Pulsatilla, over bulbs	wall, scent, evergreen ground cover
Veronica rockery speedwell	○	d	10-40 cm (4-16 in) mat	LSP-MA blue, red	Alyssum, Achillea, over bulbs	ground cover, low-growing species and varieties

○ = sun, ◑ = semi-shade, ● = shade,
d = dry, m = moist, l = likes lime, a = likes acid
ESP = early spring; MSP = mid spring; LSP = late spring, S = summer; A = autumn; W = winter

15

Saxifrage.

Elegant flowers, interesting leaves

Shady positions do not produce quite such a glowing firework display of colour as sunnier sites. Rockery plants that prefer a more humid, semi-shady to shady position display a more delicate elegance.

Delicate, elegant foam flowers.

Wake-robin.

Hosta.

Cowslips.

Bleeding heart.

Hart's tongue fern.

Leaves may also add interesting aspects to a garden area. This is particularly noticeable in a shady position. Ferns, with their long, feathery leaves, often showing attractive spore patterns on the undersides, can seem to have come straight from a primordial forest. Hosta are characterized by splendidly variegated leaves – green-white, green-yellow or even greenish-blue.

A rockery biotope

Plants for shady positions

Name	Position	Soil	Shapes of growth Height in cm/in	Flowering time Colour	Neighbouring plants	Comments
Ajuga reptans bugle	○–◐	m	15 cm (6 in) mat	MSP-LSP blue, white	Geum, Lysimachia Prunella, Scilla	beside water, ground cover
Alchemilla lady's mantle	○–◐	m	15-30 cm (6-12 in) bushy	ES-MS yellow	Campanula, Gentiana, Lysimachia	decorative foliage, ground cover
Anemone anemone ☠	◐	d	15-40 cm (6-16 in) mat	MSP-ES white, blue	Epimedium, Primula, Pulmonaria, ferns	dies back in summer, ground cover
Arabis procurrens rock cress	◐	d	10 cm (4 in) mat	ESP-LSP white	Campanula, Corydalis, Chiastophyllum	walls, evergreen
Aruncus aethusifolius goat's beard	⊙–◐	d	30 cm (12 in) bushy	LSP-ES white	Primula, Saxifraga, Polygonum	attractive foliage, autumn colours, seedheads
Astilbe chinensis astilbe	◐–◐	m	25-40 cm (10-16 in) bushy	LS-EA pink	Lysimachia, grasses ferns	seedheads, low-growing species, ground cover
Bergenia hybrids large-leaved saxifrage	○–◐	m	30-40 cm (12-16 in) bushy	MSP-LSP/MA pink, white	Saxifraga, grasses, ferns	coloured leaves, evergreen
Brunnera macrophylla perennial forget-me-not	○–◐	m	40 cm (16 in) bushy	MSP-LSP blue	Doronicum, Primula, Epimedium, tulips	ground cover
Corydalis lutea yellow corydalis	⊙–◐	d	20 cm (8 in) bushy	LSP-MA yellow	Arabis, Linaria, ferns	walls, ground cover
Dicentra eximia bleeding heart	◐	m	20 cm (8 in) bushy	LSP-MS red, white	Heucherella, Tiarella, Viola, grasses, ferns	decorative foliage
Doronicum orientale leopard's bane	○–◐	d	25-40 cm (10-16 in) bushy	MSP-LSP yellow	Brunnera, tulips	dies back in summer
Epimedium barrenwort (bishop's hat)	◐	m	20 cm (8 in) bushy	MSP-LSP yellow, red	Dicentra, Anemone, grasses, ferns	autumn colour, evergreen, ground cover
Euphorbia spurge ☠	◐–●	d l	20-50 cm (8-20 in) mat	MSP-LSP yellow	Anemone, Geranium	decorative foliage autumn colour
Geranium crane's bill	○–◐	d	15-40 cm (6-16 in) bushy	MS-EA red, blue	Campanula, Alchemilla, grasses, ferns, woody plants	autumn colour, ground cover
Geum avens	○–◐	f	30 cm (12 in) bushy	LSP-LS yellow, red	Heucherella, Viola, Brunnera, Primula	
Helleborus hybridus ☠ Christmas or Lenten rose	◐–●	m l	20-40 cm (8-16 in) bushy	MW-LSP red, pink	Brunnera, Anemone, Primula, Pulmonaria	evergreen
Heucherella tiarelloides coral flower	◐–●	m	40 cm (16 in) bushy	ES-LS pink	Dicentra, Saxifraga, grasses	autumn colour, ground cover
Hosta hosta	◐–●	m	40 cm (16 in) bushy	MS-LS white, lilac	Campanula, Astilbe, Primula, grasses	decorative foliage, low-growing species and varieties
Lamium maculatum spotted deadnettle	◐–●	m	15 cm (6 in) trailing	LSP-LS red, lilac	Pulmonaria, grasses	decorative foliage, ground cover
Omphalodes verna navelwort (blue-eyed Mary)	◐–●	m	10 cm (4 in) mat	MSP-LSP blue, white	Dicentra, Primula, Waldsteinia, woody plants	ground cover
Polygonum affinum knotweed	○–●	m	20 cm (8 in) mat	MS-EA pink	Alchemilla, Hosta, Campanula, Inula	ground cover

Plants for shady positions

Name	Position	Soil	Shapes of growth Height in cm/in	Flowering time Colour	Neighbouring plants	Comments
Primula primrose	◐–●	m	10-40 cm (4-16 in) bushy	ESP-MS multi-coloured	*Anemone, Brunnera, Viola, Tiarella, Pulmonaria*	
Prunella grandiflora self-heal	○–◐	m	20 cm (8 in) mat	MS-EA lilac, white	*Campanula, Inula,*	ground cover
Pulmonaria lungwort	◐–●	m	30 cm (12 in) bushy	ESP-MSP blue, red	*Helleborus,* ferns	white/coloured varieties
Saxifraga saxifrage	○–◐	m l	15-30 cm (6-12 in) mat	MSP-MA pink, yellow	*Omphalodes, Bergenia, Dicentra,* grasses, ferns	autumn colours, evergreen
Tiarella foam flower	◐–●	m	20 cm (8 in) mat	LSP-MS white	*Aruncus, Dicentra, Primula,* grasses	autumn colours, evergreen, ground cover
Trillium wake-robin	◐–●	m	20-40 cm (8-16 in) bushy	MSP-LSP white, red	*Omphalodes, Waldsteinia*	decorative foliage
Viola violet	○–◐	d	15 cm (6 in) mat	ESP-MSP/LSP-EA purple	various varieties mixed *Primula,* grasses	ground cover
Waldsteinia	◐–●	d	15 cm (6 in) mat	MSP-LSP yellow	*Helleborus, Viola, Pulmonaria*	ground cover

Grasses and ferns

Name	Position	Soil	Shapes of growth Height in cm/in	Flowering time Colour	Neighbouring plants	Comments
Carex true sedge	○–◐	m l	15-40 cm (6-16 in) bushy	ESP-MS	*Helleborus, Lamium, Tiarella*	ground cover
Deschampsia cespitosa	○–◐	m	60 cm (24 in)	ES-LS bushy	*Hosta, Primula, Saxifraga*	ground cover
Luzula rush	◐	d	20-40 cm (8-16 in) bushy	MSP-MS	*Hosta, Heucherella, Prunella, Viola,*	ground cover
Asplenium trichomanes	◐–●	m l	10 cm (4 in) mat		*Saxifraga, Chorydalis*	wall, evergreen
Blechnum spicant hard fern	◐–●	m l	40 cm (16 in) bushy		*Helleborus, Geranium, Pulmonaria*	ground cover, evergreen
Dryopteris buckler fern	◐–●	m	40 cm (16 in) bushy		*Epimedium, Geranium*	low-growing varieties
Phyllitis hart's tongue fern	◐–●	m l	40 cm (16 in) mat		*Dicentra, Helleborus, Saxifraga*	wall, evergreen
Polypodium fern	●	m a	20-30 cm (8-12 in) bushy		*Geranium, Pulmonaria, Saxifraga*	evergreen
Polystichum fern	●–◐	m	30-50 cm (12-20 in) bushy		*Chorydalis, Epimedium*	

○ = sun, ◐ = semi-shade, ● = shade,
d = dry, m = moist, l = likes lime, a = likes acid
ESP = early spring; MSP = mid spring; LSP = late spring, S = summer; A = autumn; W = winter

Planning

What could be more beautiful than a rockery that is covered in flowers all year round? Careful planning is essential if you wish to ensure that you have such an eyecatching feature in your garden. Our flowering calendar will help you to choose the right plants.

Above: The flowers of the pink look really fragile.
Left: Many rockery plants seem to thrive in barren, stony surroundings.

Correct planning

Landscape design

The soil that is excavated when a house is being built, plus broken bits of stone, is excellent for landscape modelling.

Even on plots of ground that have already been designed you can still make some alterations. Digging out a pond can often create sufficient quantities of soil to construct a rockery. You may also be able to create sunken sitting areas or terraced paths across gentle slopes.

Proceed slowly and step by step when removing a mature stand of trees as this will give any wildlife time to find other shelter. For similar reasons, do not do this work during nesting time. Individual remaining bushes will provide variation in your rockery. Groups of herbaceous perennials left along the edges look good as a background feature.

Choice of position

Soil preparation begins with the choice of a suitable position. A careful study of all the areas of the garden is very important for this. Sloping positions are wonderful natural terrain for rockery design, but even level areas in a front garden or close to a patio can be planted effectively with rockery plants.

Preparing the soil

Good soil preparation is a prerequisite in the creation of an easy-to-care-for planting.

Soil analysis: First, try to determine the structure of the soil. Sandy soil will sift easily through your fingers; loamy soils are stickier and can be shaped; clay-rich soils are very hard and often lumpy. You can determine the mineral content with the help of a tester kit from the gardening trade or you can send soil samples to a specialist laboratory for soil analysis. The lime content of soil is particularly important when choosing rockery plants. The lime content determines the pH factor, or degree of acidity, of the soil. Soils with a high lime content (alkaline soils) have a pH factor over 7. Acid soils contain little or no lime. Their pH value will be less than 7. Soil with a pH of 7 is considered to be neutral.

Removing weeds: The thorough elimination of all weeds, together with their roots, is absolutely essential when creating a rockery or any other bed. Dig over the bed with a garden fork and remove any large masses of roots. Using a spade would only result in chopping the roots up. In the case of very badly weed-infested areas, it is a good idea to allow the bed to lie fallow for a few months after digging over. Then you will be able to eliminate newly grown weeds more easily.

NB: Even the smallest fragments of roots of couch grass, ground elder (*Aegopodium podagraria*) or field bindweed (*Convolvulus arvensis*) will grow into new plants. Once weed roots have become entwined with rockery plant roots, the only option is to dig them all out and replace the plants. Even the rockery plants themselves can turn into weeds. Among vigorously growing rockery plants, one can often find rampaging species that are only suitable for planting designs in large areas.

Installing drainage: If your soil is very compacted or rich in clay, you should definitely install a drainage layer. Dig out the top layer of soil to about two spades' depth down. Fill the pit with a 10-20 cm (4-8 in) thick layer of stones, coarse gravel or broken bricks. Then replace some of the humus layer. You can also mix small quantities of sand and smaller particles of rubble in with the humus. The conditions for rockery plants will be ideal in a bed prepared in this way.

NB: If your soil is very sandy, inserting a water-absorbing layer is highly recommended. For this purpose, use a loamy sub-layer of the sort of soil that might have been dug out when excavations took place before the house was built.

Improving the soil: Use garden compost and a small quantity of hoof and horn chips as a controlled-release fertilizer under the topsoil (see p. 51).

Probably the easiest way to construct a rockery is on a plot of ground where a new house has just been built. Later on, moving large quantities of earth or transporting in extra soil is an expensive and difficult undertaking.
Here, snow-in-summer (Cerastium) is tumbling luxuriantly out of a rockery.

Choosing and laying rocks and stones

Next to the actual plants, rocks and stones are the most important design element of a rockery. They not only influence the appearance of the rockery but will also become an integral part of the biotope. You must always take into consideration all the naturally occurring conditions in your garden when choosing stones or rocks.

Choosing rocks and stones

There are many different types, shapes and colours of rocks and stones. If you decide to use rocks and stones from the immediate vicinity of your garden, you will definitely not go wrong. If you are planning a small rockery, you might be able to talk owners of fields into letting you choose and take away stones or rocks that you find piled up along the edges of fields. In the case of a larger design or a drystone wall, it is better to turn to a local quarry or a firm that sells natural stone. Larger quantities of stone or rock will not be cheap; nor will their transportation.

The type of stone is determined by the soil conditions. Stones and rocks will weather, crumble and disappear into the soil where plants will absorb their mineral content.
● Alkaline-loving plants grow on lime-rich soil.
● Basalt, granite or sandstone will be found on neutral or acid soils.
My tip: It is, of course, possible to influence the pH value of weak acid soils by using limestone in the composition of your rockery. The choice of plants then becomes even greater. The soil should, however, also be improved with additional generous quantities of garden compost and lime.

The shapes of rocks and stones you choose should be determined by the design of your rockery.
● large, beautifully shaped stones for groups of natural rocks;
● flat stones for drystone walls (see p. 38);
● level, non-slip stones for stepping stones through the rockery.
The colours of rocks and stones will be determined by the conditions on site and also by your own taste.
● Light-coloured stones look friendly and are recommended for shady gardens.
● Dark-coloured stones look a little gloomy. In very sunny positions dark or black stones will store a great deal of heat.

1 Lay all stones broadest surface down.

2 For gardens on slopes it is preferable to build in small steps; soil is easily washed away from a sloping surface.

3 When creating random stone groups, partially sink the stones into the soil to prevent them from slipping.

Not all plants will cope with such heat as it is released.

Laying rocks and stones

(illustration 1)

The basic rule is that, in nature, rocks and stones always lie on their broadest flat surface (see illustration 1). Sharp, jagged-looking stones will look quite unnatural. Groups of rocks and stones of different sizes combined with smaller groups of plants or single shrubs will look very natural. A large stone can be partially or almost completely covered with plants.

Tips on laying rocks and stones

(illustrations 2-4)

Depending on the design of your rockery, there are certain points to bear in mind when choosing and laying stones.

Miniature rockeries: Do not use very large stones or rocks for smaller, level rockery beds. Instead, you could create a flat mound, for example.

Sloping rockery (see illustration 2): Following a natural example is particularly important for this type of bed. Create small hollows on the slope for larger stones and then plant your plants later on as if they had caught hold of the stone. You can also group smaller stones around larger ones. As far as possible, avoid creating sloping areas of soil. By digging soil steps and laying stones skilfully, you can achieve a terraced effect on a natural slope.

Groups of random stones: You can choose very large stones for this design. When laying them, try to achieve a totally natural effect.

NB: Don't forget about safety! Very large rocks or stones should be partly sunk into the soil. Stones that tip or slide, which is quite possible after heavy rainfall, could prove a source of accidents.

Rockeries with water: A pool or small pond should always be positioned at the lowest point of the terrain. Running water will always eventually round off and smooth stones. Bizarre shapes or rocks with sharp edges look unnatural.

Sunken paths will provide ideal conditions of growth for the most varied plants. Such paths can be a fascinating design element in a rockery garden.

4 A sunken pathway can be installed at the lowest point of the terrain where sloping gardens rise up on both sides.

Correct planning

Careful planning brings success

You should spend some time on planning your rockery. A well-planned rockery bed will save you unnecessary expense on costly plants, failures and disappointments, growing the wrong plants together and frequent replanting. Plants that look natural and decorative are recommended. From the huge range of available plants, you are certain to find something to satisfy your taste for colour and shape. Natural-looking, harmoniously combined rockery plants will prove an eyecatching feature at any time of year.

Colourful splendour is the result of careful initial planning.

Compiling plant lists

Consider the conditions in your garden. What is the soil like? Is the chosen plot sunny or shady? Once you have clarified these points, you can make your choice with the help of the plant tables on pages 14 and 18. For this table, I have selected and compiled particularly decorative, gardener-friendly rockery plants and also suggested suitable companion plants that require the same conditions. These varieties will usually be readily obtainable in nurseries with good selections.

You may, of course, already have some of the plants you want to use in your garden or you may be able to get a few rockery plants from friends or neighbours. Many people have particular favourites that they would like to add to their garden. In that case, I recommend selecting plants according to companion plants that look good together and will require the same conditions. Good plant catalogues will generally give you sound advice. There are suitable companion plants for every combination, which will work well together and look effective, perhaps because they have the same flowering time, harmoniously blending colours or attractive leaf structures.

Remember that successful plant communities will closely mimic natural environmental conditions and that companion plants must also go well with other neighbouring plants. Soon you will have a long plant list. Write down the names of all the rockery plants that you think are necessary for your rockery and that you like. Add to this list the flowering times, flower colours, height of growth and shape of growth. You should aim to have both cushion-shaped and mat-shaped rockery plants as well as taller and bushy species in fairly equal numbers, depending on the size of your rockery bed.

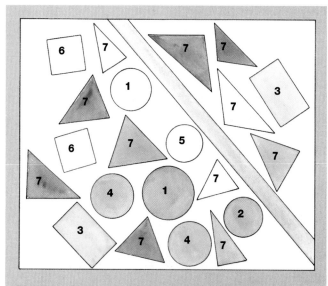

Planting plan for the photograph on page 26
Symbols and colours
Squares: flowering time from early to late spring.
Rectangles: flowering time from late spring to mid summer.
Circles: flowering time from early to late summer.
Triangles: flowering time from late summer to mid autumn.

1 pink (Dianthus gratianapolitanus); 2 thyme (Thymus citriodorus "Golden Dwarf"); 3 Campanula carpatica; 4 thrift (Armeria maritima); 5 Antennaria parviflora; 6 perennial candytuft (Iberis saxatilis); 7 thyme (Thymus serphyllum).

Sorting according to flowering time and colour

Now sort this plant list into a table that corresponds to a flowering calendar (see p. 30). You should also note any particular features of the plants before you make your final choices. If a certain colour appears to be missing during a particular flowering phase, you can add more plants. If you have too many similar species, you will probably be able to find some companion plants in the plant lists.

Making planting plans

Method
● First make a drawing of the bed, preferably according to scale. Draw in the cardinal points and the direction of any slope.
● Using coloured paper, cut out the respective colour symbols for the different flowering colours and for different flowering times (see illustration left). The size of the symbols should represent the space required in the bed.
● Write the plant names on the paper symbols.
● Move the coloured bits of paper around on the drawing until you have found the right positions for all the plants.
● Glue the symbols to your drawing.
You now have a finished, workable planting plan.
My tip: Keep your planting plan in a transparent envelope. It will be your most important aid to planting.
NB: It is advisable to divide plants into leader plants, companion plants and filler plants (see p. 28). Rockery plants that remain tidy all year round, such as evergreen and autumn-flowering species, should be employed more in the foreground.

Buying and planting

Plant requirements
(illustration 1)

You will find suggested figures for the number of plants to plant per square metre or yard in plant catalogues, or else you can obtain advice from someone in the gardening trade. If you have decided to make do with a smaller number of plants to begin with, perhaps for reasons of cost (many rockery plants are not cheap), you will need a bit of patience. Summer annuals can make inexpensive stopgaps for the first few years. Also remember that plants need friendly neighbours in order to thrive (see illustration 1). The ratio will be determined by a leader plant (tallest plant): secondary plants (low-growing species): ground-cover plants or gap fillers. While you will require only single specimens of the leader plants, you will need larger numbers of the companion plants and fillers. You should be able to estimate your plant requirements when planning the rockery bed.

Tips on buying

You will usually find expert advice in a plant nursery but there are a few points to consider for yourself.
● Only purchase plants with detailed labels. Missing labels or those with insufficient information may diguise species that will go on a rampage and soon take over your entire rockery.
● Check for infestation with pests and diseases or for compost full of weeds. These are all signs of insufficient care and attention.
● Have a good look at the plant compost. Plants grown in pure peat are often grown for mass production. They will find it very hard to adapt to alien conditions in a garden.

Planting time

Generally speaking, rockery plants in containers can be planted all year round. Only when the ground is frozen or the weather is very dry and hot should you refrain from planting. The best planting time for a newly built rockery is spring or autumn. In the spring, however, always remember that there could be late frosts and newly planted rockery plants may require protective covering. In the autumn, do not leave planting too late. The plants should have established themselves in their new environment before the first heavy

1 *The tallest plants set the tone. Some slightly smaller companion plants have been added. Empty spaces can be filled with small rockery plants.*

frosts. Choose a dull day, perhaps after rain. The soil will then be loose and easier to press down around the plant. Very wet soil, particularly heavy soils, are unsuitable for planting.

How to plant
(illustrations 2a-2d)

First stand the rockery plants, still in their pots, in a bath of water (see illustration 2a). This will enable the rootstocks to absorb plenty of moisture.
Now consult your planting plan and distribute the plants, still in their pots, over the well-prepared rockery bed. This way, you can still correct any positioning that doesn't look quite right. Keep moving them around until you are happy with the result but don't deviate too much from your planting plan without considering such points as height and colour combinations. Alter your planting plan before you go ahead with major changes. When planting, work in the following sequence:

leader plants first, then companion plants, finally fillers. Do not plant the rockery plants in a row but, rather, put together loose groups of plants. Make sure that gaps are left between the plants of one variety that are planted together.
● Carefully loosen up the rootstocks a little (see illustration 2b).
● Now dig a sufficiently large planting hole for each plant.
● Moisten the soil a little and then plant each plant (see illustration 2c).
NB: Do not set the plants any deeper in the soil than they were in their pots.
● Firmly press the soil down around the roots and water thoroughly (see illustration 2d).
● After watering, you may have to press the soil down again. Afterwards, check daily that the soil around the plant is sufficiently moist. Only water if the soil is very dry. Too much water may harm your plants. Small, new leaves will indicate that a rockery plant is thriving and growing properly. If you decide to plant in the autumn,

2a The rootstock can absorb water when immersed in a bath.

2b The rootstock is loosened up before planting.

2c The soil should be pressed down after planting.

2d Thoroughly water the newly planted plant.

you will have to wait until the spring for new shoots to indicate that all is well.
My tip: Leave the labels on any new plants when planting a new rockery. This will help you to locate even the smallest varieties later on. Also hang on to your planting plan and make notes of

any changes to it. It's a good idea later on, in spring, summer and autumn, to take photographs of the rockery bed and compare these with your plan. The photographs should enable you to spot gaps or places where colour is lacking.

Correct planning

Calendar of flowering times

Season	ESP	MSP	LSP	ES	MS	LS	EA	LA
white								
○		Arabis caucasica			Anaphalis		seedheads	
			Gypsophila repens					
	Iberis saxatilis			Dryas octopetala		seedheads		
			Cerastium tomentosum			Carlina		
			Antennaria		Leontopodium alpinum			
◐	Arabis procurrens					Prunella grandiflora		
			Dicentra eximia					
			Aruncus aethusifolius			seedheads pink/leaf colour		
		Saxifraga arendsii		Saxifraga umbrosa		Saxifraga cortusifolia		
●	Helleborus		Tiarella wherryi					
yellow								
○		Iris barbata-nana			Helianthemum hybrids			
			Alyssum saxatile	Sedum reflexum				
		Potentilla verna "Nana"						
						Oenothera missouriensis		
◐		Euphorbia polychroma			Inula ensifolia			
	Primula		Corydalis lutea					
		Doronicum		Alchemilla mollis				
		Epimedium				Sedum kamtschaticum		
●		Waldsteinia		Geum bulgaricum				
		Euphorbia amygdaloides						

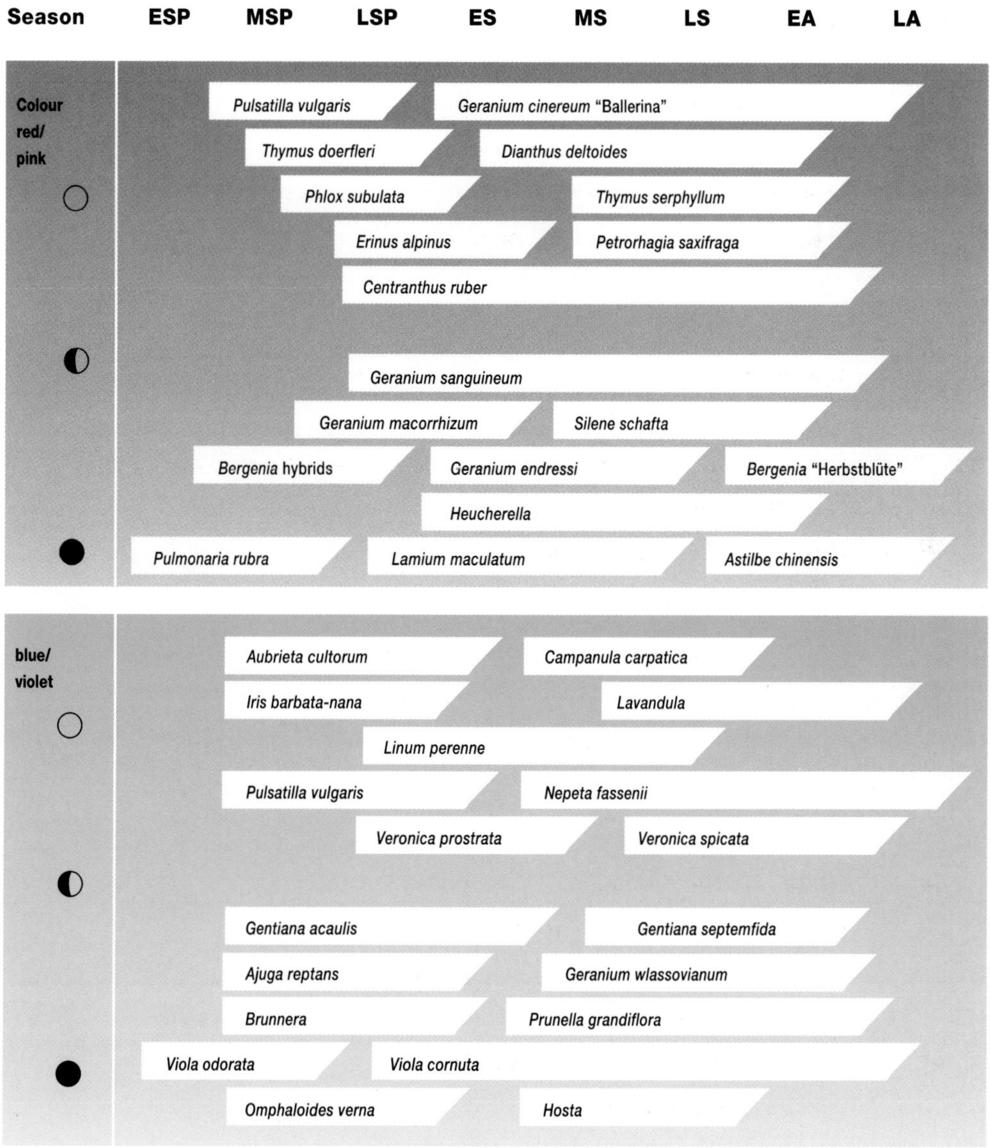

Season	ESP	MSP	LSP	ES	MS	LS	EA	LA

Colour red/pink

○
- Pulsatilla vulgaris
- Geranium cinereum "Ballerina"
- Thymus doerfleri
- Dianthus deltoides
- Phlox subulata
- Thymus serphyllum
- Erinus alpinus
- Petrorhagia saxifraga
- Centranthus ruber

◐
- Geranium sanguineum
- Geranium macrorrhizum
- Silene schafta
- Bergenia hybrids
- Geranium endressi
- Bergenia "Herbstblüte"
- Heucherella

●
- Pulmonaria rubra
- Lamium maculatum
- Astilbe chinensis

blue/violet

○
- Aubrieta cultorum
- Campanula carpatica
- Iris barbata-nana
- Lavandula
- Linum perenne
- Pulsatilla vulgaris
- Nepeta fassenii
- Veronica prostrata
- Veronica spicata

◐
- Gentiana acaulis
- Gentiana septemfida
- Ajuga reptans
- Geranium wlassovianum
- Brunnera
- Prunella grandiflora

●
- Viola odorata
- Viola cornuta
- Omphaloides verna
- Hosta

ESP = early spring; MSP = mid spring; LSP = late spring; S = summer; A = autumn; W = winter

A multitude of ideas

A rockery can be built in any garden, in a sunny or shady position, taking up a large or small area. If you want to make your rockery a bit unusual, you can even design it along a stream or round a pond. Scented plants will create a romantic atmosphere.

Above: Campanula auchori.
Left: Cheerful poppies on a drystone wall with snow-in-summer and thrift.

A multitude of ideas

Miniature rockeries

Space is often at a premium around the entrance to a garden and around the patio of small gardens. Here, even small rockery beds with attractive leaves and flowers can become an eyecatching feature.

Make special features of small beds

This kind of bed is seen almost with a bird's-eye view by the observer. Small rockeries are also accessible from all sides and can, therefore, show off the most varied range and harmony of colour. It is easy to incorporate highlights for every season. It is also a good idea to choose evergreen species for such a bed, perhaps with some attractive seedstands, so that it does not become too boring in the winter. Rockery plants that have a long flowering time, or flower several times, and which look decorative from all sides are particularly recommended in small beds. The following species can be used to achieve permanent flowering in many colours.
● In a sunny position: crane's bill species (*Geranium cinereum*, *G. sanguineum*), *Gypsophila*, rock cinquefoil (*Potentilla*), red valerian (*Centranthus*).
● In semi-shade or shade: corydalis (*Corydalis lutea*),

pansies, variegated deadnettle (*Lamium maculatum* "Silbergroschen").
The following have a second flowering phase in late summer or early autumn after pruning: rock rose (*Helianthemum*), *Campanula portenschlagiana*, pinks, thrift (*Armeria*).
For restricted spaces, I recommend choosing more delicate species that go well with other plants. These dwarf rockery plants generally grow very slowly. If you aim for a large number of plants during the first year, you will be able to achieve a wealth of plants and flowers. Three rockery plants of one species, planted at the right spacing, will ensure a dense, luxuriant carpet of plants. More patient gardeners may make do with just one of each plant. Financial considerations do, of course, play a part in this as well as the small, slow-growing species, in particular, are not cheap. Any gaps can be skilfully filled with delicate annual summer flowers; for example, alyssum, perennial candytuft (*Iberis*) or lobelia.

Design ideas for mini rockeries

A few planting examples for various times of the year may encourage you to experiment further when designing your own beds. Depending on the size and

type of rockery you wish to create, try to plant groups that will flower at the same times and put together combinations of rockery plants that will create focal points at different times of year.
A raised bed, perhaps incorporated into the patio, is an attractive possibility when designing a small rockery. Plants that like dry conditions are particularly good for planting here.
Planting examples
● *A miniature heathland garden*
Choose different heathers for a miniature heathland garden, especially evergreen *Erica carnea* and *Erica tetralix* varieties. *Calluna* species can be planted individually between these as they look less tidy in the spring. Plants that are good for combining include pasque flower (*Pulsatilla*), thyme, pinks, *Antennaria*, pearly everlasting (*Anaphalis*) and grasses.
NB: Make sure that drainage is adequate and that the soil is not rich in lime as *Calluna* and *Erica tetralix* do not like lime.
● *Gravel bed*
Do not plant heather species in a gravel bed. Instead, use other rockery plants that can tolerate dry conditions like *Eriophyllum lanatum*, rock rose, lavender and *Inula*.
Various *Sedum* species are ideal as ground-cover plants.
This kind of bed can also be created on lime-rich soils.

Small flowering islands can give a paved patio an inviting appearance. Just leave out a few paving stones at intervals when laying the patio or remove single larger paving slabs. The plants will then grow over the edges of the paving and any angular contours will be disguised, giving the whole a natural appearance. A few tiny plants will soon colonize even the smallest cracks all by themselves to create flowering spots in previously bare places.

Planting examples
● Spring – perennial candytuft (*Iberis saxatilis*), pasque flower (*Pulsatilla*), gentian (*Gentiana acaulis*), primrose.
● Early summer – *Gypsophila repens*, rock rose, crane's bill (*Geranium cinereum*).
● Summer – edelweiss, *Sedum album*, thyme (*Thymus serphyllum*), grasses.

● Autumn – carline thistle (*Carlina*), *Inula ensifolia*, *Sedum cauticulum*.

Groups of, or individual, rocks or stones also look very attractive. In the middle of an area of lawn, surrounded by grasses, ferns or flowering herbaceous plants, a group of rocks can look very natural.

My tip: Choose stones with indentations or hollows in which you can plant small rock plants.

Planting examples
● *Sunny position*
For planting among stones try houseleek (*Sempervivum*), *Sedum* species, cushion thyme, *Petrorhagia saxifraga*, *Heliosperma alpestre*. Grasses, lavender, rock rose, red valerian, flax and cat mint also look very good between or beside stones.
● *Shady position*
Saxifraga species, *Corydalis*, flax (*Linaria cymbalaria*) and ferns can be planted in moist hollows in stones. Larger ferns combined with bleeding heart, dwarf honeysuckle and *Bergenia* look very effective at the foot of a large stone.

A tufa stone covered in colourful flowering plants.

A multitude of ideas

Sunny slopes

In the desire to achieve an abundance of easy-to-care-for greenery, it is all too tempting to plant fast-growing species like dwarf cotoneaster and potentilla on sunny slopes. In the long term, however, plantings of such species are neither beautiful nor easy to care for. Eventually, only rigorous intervention with clippers and a saw will be able to bring order in the veritable thicket you have created. Huge quantities of clippings will result, which will defeat any hope of composting.

Sunny slopes planted with colourful rockery plants will bring much more variety to most gardens. When designing slopes, two possibilities offer themselves: a natural slope or an architecturally designed slope (see p. 43).

A natural slope

It is quite possible to create a natural slope just like a sunny mountain slope. Aided by stones, the roots of the plants will soon dig deep into the soil.

NB: Think about future gardening chores even when planting. Flat, natural stone slabs that blend in harmoniously make excellent stepping stones when chores have to be done (see laying stones, p. 25; steps and paths, p. 42).

A planting example in cheerful colours:

The following flowering combination in many different colours is very attractive in a large area on a sunny slope. Pasque flowers (*Pulsatilla*) in red, white and violet; wild tulips; crocuses; thyme (*Thymus doerfleri*); alyssum; rockery speedwell (*Veronica prostrata*) in white and blue; rock rose in white, yellow or red; *Campanula carpatica* in blue or white; dwarf inula; carline thistle (*Carlina acaulis*), thyme (*Thymus serphyllum*) in red or white; rockery speedwell (*Veronica spicata*); grasses.

Method

● First distribute the taller species, like rock rose, dwarf inula and rockery speedwell (*Veronica spicata*) individually or in small groups over the area.

● Carline thistle and pasque flower should be added singly to these groups. Alyssum and campanula look very decorative next to large stones.

● Ground-covering thyme and speedwell should be planted in larger groups over bulbs. They will soon cover the whole surface of the soil and smother many of the stones with their colourful flowering cushions.

Delicate grasses will provide lively accents, even in winter, beside the seedstands of carline thistle and the evergreen rockery plants.

Larger plants will bring more variety to large sloping areas. The following species of herbaceous plants are just as suitable for sunny rockeries: *Centaurea*, large daisies, *Erigeron*, summer asters, cushion asters, *Coreopsis*, sage species, *Limonium*, *Rudbeckia*.

Small flowering shrubs and dwarf conifers are also good for breaking up large natural slopes. Dwarf berberis, summer lilac, broom species, *Caryopteris*, *Ruta*, St John's wort, juniper species or dwarf pines are all ideal as such colourful designs require as quiet a background as possible. Neutral house walls make a good backdrop in a front garden but such a variety of colours will also look good in front of a regularly clipped hedge. Herbaceous plant combinations in two colours have a more tranquil, but still equally attractive, effect on smaller areas of slopes.

A planting example in red/yellow: Plants in brilliant colours look dazzling in front of dark conifers.

● Spring – phlox (*Phlox subulata*) in red; alyssum in yellow.

● Early summer – pinks (*Dianthus gratianapolitanus*) in red; flax (*Linum flavum*) in yellow.

● Summer – rock cinquefoil (*Potentilla atrosanguinea* "Gibson's Scarlet") in red; rock rose in yellow.

You can combine these with *Coryopsis* and *Rudbeckia* as well

A sunny slope with luxuriant flowers all year round

as with broom and berberis species.

Planting example in blue-lilac-white: Plants with silvery foliage and pastel-coloured flowers will create a romantic atmosphere in your garden. They will also give the illusion of more space in the smallest area.

● Spring – aubrieta in blue; rock cress in white look most effective.
● Early summer – snow-in-

summer in white can be simple but luxurious too.

● Summer – cat mint in blue; valerian (*Centranthus ruber* "Albus") in white creates a very pretty picture.
● Autumn – pearly everlasting (*Anaphalis*) in white creates a dreamy, atmospheric mood. Suitable woody species and shrubs: *Ruta* and *Caryopteris*, sage species, *Limonium* and

Echinopsis, *Yucca* and taller grasses. Naturally, these look best in a larger space.

Building a drystone wall

Drystone walls make beautiful features in gardens, whether they are free standing (see illustration 1) or support a slope (see illustration 2). Many rockery plants feel right at home in the cracks in such a wall, while tiny creatures will also find room to sun themselves or to take shelter.

Preparations

The best time to build drystone walls is early spring or autumn. A light protective covering of conifer brushwood is recommended for winter protection.

Materials

● Flat stones are easiest to fit together in walls. A large heap of stones is recommended so that you can harmoniously fit together stones of different sizes. Smaller stones can be used as filling material for cracks and crevices. You can also build walls out of differently shaped, random stones. With a little patience, you will be able to fit the stones together like a jigsaw puzzle.

● Cement or mortar is not a suitable binding material for a drystone wall. A mixture of two-thirds lime or loamy or even clay-rich garden soil and one-third cow dung is the best binding material. This mixture is easiest to work with if it is slightly moist.

My tip: Dried-up cow pats from a meadow are better for this job than stable manure which contains too much straw and would endanger stability. Your local farmer should not object to you collecting cow dung from his fields. If you are unable to obtain cow dung, bought cattle dung compost makes a possible substitute. Cow dung is an excellent binding material and will also serve as a controlled-release fertilizer for the plants in the wall.

● You should already have purchased your plants before you start building the drystone wall. Planting them later on is less satisfactory as long roots are difficult to push deep between the stones. The stones and the plants should be "built" together in one working procedure.

The foundation of the drystone wall

For a maximum height of not more than 1 m (40 in), you can build a drystone wall without a concrete foundation.

● Dig out a trench following a string drawn out to mark the course of the wall.
A width of 50 cm (20 in) and a depth of 30-50 cm (12-20 in) will be

1 A freestanding drystone wall that slopes on both sides.

2 A supporting drystone wall also requires a good foundation.

3 Irregularly shaped stones can be fitted together like jigsaw puzzle pieces.

4 Push the roots deep between the stones.

sufficient for a 1 m (40 in) high wall. Very flat walls can be built without foundations.

● In sandy soil you should install a gravel layer as a foundation. A gravel or rubble layer is also recommended for drainage when building on heavy soils.

● Start building the wall below the surface of the soil. Use the largest stones for this to give the wall a firm base.

● Fill the cracks with loamy soil which can be washed in with a vigorous stream of water. Cow dung will not be needed for the foundation. Any air pockets left could cause slippage later.

Building the wall
(illustrations 3 and 4)

● Choose the largest stones for the bottom layers.

● Avoid any cross joins. The stones should be laid alternately as in building a house wall (see illustration 3).

● The cross section of the wall is shaped like a truncated cone. Drystone walls that are intended to provide support for a slope should be built inclining against the slope. The slope of the wall should be such that for each metre (yard) of walling, the wall should fall 15 cm (6 in) against the slope.

● The joins should also gradually incline towards the wall or towards the

centre of the wall.

● The centre of free-standing drystone walls should be filled with rubble, gravel, small stones and soil. Leaning walls are also filled in the same way.

● Freestanding walls should have a depression running along the top of the wall. This will serve as a water reservoir.

● Insert the plants while building.

● Choose suitable cracks and spots in the wall, according to the requirements of the species of plant for growing conditions and position. The foot of the wall will be cooler and moister than the crown of the wall. The rootstocks, which you should have loosened up a little, should be surrounded with soil and pushed into the area at the back of the wall (see illustration 4).

● You should use stable, broad-based stones for the top courses of the wall. A freestanding drystone wall may replace a fence or divide up a garden.

Planting example
● sunny side – aubrieta, alyssum,

thyme species, cushion phlox, cushion pinks, gypsophila.

● shady side – saxifrage species, corydalis, *Campanula poscharskyana*, crane's bill species, violets, small ferns.

● top of the wall – houseleek species, *Sedum* species, edelweiss, pinks, yarrow, grasses.

NB: Please note the division of plants into leader plants, companion plants and filler plants (see p. 28). Rockery plants that look tidy all year round – i.e. the evergreen and autumn-flowering species – should be used more in the foreground.

A multitude of ideas

A shady rockery

All gardens have their shady spots. This does not mean, however, that these corners need be less attractive than other parts. Particularly during hot weeks in the summer, shady parts of the garden may become favourite sitting areas for the family. In the summer when the sun rises in the north east, the north side of the house can be an ideal spot for breakfasting, while in the evening hours you will still be able to enjoy the last rays of the sun here.

Combining shade-loving plants

Even among rockery plants there are some that like a less sunny position. Plants that grow on the north side of mountains will also thrive in the shade of a building. The soil will remain moist longer in the shade; in addition, the use of stones ensures that the soil will stay slightly damp, which a lot of shade-loving plants particularly like. A drystone wall is also a possibility in a shady rockery.

While many plants and flowers tend to look limp and faded in strong sunlight, shade-loving rockery plants will remain fresh and green, a factor that makes up for their often rather restrained colours.

Small bodies of water, like pools or ponds, will also provide additional humidity and increase the range of designs that can be employed.

Many grasses and ferns will thrive only in the shade. Among these, too, there are delicate species that would do well in a shady rockery.

Small shade-loving shrubs and trees are indispensable for larger rockeries. Among these are creeping and climbing spindle tree species, ivy, holly, *Kerria*, mountain laurel (*Kalmia*), mahonia, rhododendron species, privet, snowball and yew. Evergreen species can be used as a background or visual screen in rockeries. Combined with sun-loving species, they will form a harmonious transition to other parts of the garden. Many bulbous plants can also liven up the soil under woody plants; for example, winter aconite (*Eranthis*), snowdrops and scilla. Taller rockery plants are equally suitable for combining in rockeries; for example, monkshood (*Aconitum napellus*), taller astilbe species, foxglove (*Digitalis*), honeysuckle, tall campanula, *Cimicifuga* and aquilegia.

Planting example: a drystone wall in the shade.

- Spring – foam flower, navelwort (*Omphalodes verna*).
- Early summer – yellow corydalis, *Campanula poscharskyana*.
- Summer – flax, planted with crane's bill (*Geranium endressi*).
- Autumn – self-heal (*Prunella grandiflora*), astilbe.
- Winter – evergreen rockery plants, ferns.

Planting example: leaves in the shade.

Try out a design incorporating the most varied leaf colours and shapes. Variegated foliage, in particular white or yellow patterned, is a special feature of shade-loving plants. Herbaceous plants or small shrubs with flowers in delicate shades of white, light pink, light lilac or yellow will bring elegance to your shady area.

- plants with variegated leaves – *Hosta undulata*, *Hosta fortunei* "Aurea", variegated deadnettle (*Lamium maculatum* "White Nancy"), lungwort (*Pulmonaria officinalis* "Sissinghurst White"), saxifrage (*Saxifraga umbrosa* "Aureopunctata").
- small shrubs with variegated leaves – spindleberry bush, ivy (*Hedera helix* "Goldherz"), periwinkle (*Vinca major* "Variegata").
- white or yellow-flowering rockery plants with beautiful leaves and partially coloured foliage in the autumn – lady's mantle, dwarf honeysuckle, yellow corydalis, bleeding heart, Christmas rose, wake-robin (*Trillium grandiflorum*), pansy (*Viola cornuta* "White Perfection"), grasses and ferns.

Beautiful rockery gardens can be grown even in shady positions.

A multitude of ideas

Designing steps and paths

You can give your garden a very individual look with flowering paths and steps.

Paths at lawn edges can be made of sunken natural stone slabs that form a boundary for the rockery bed on the lawn side. Plants that grow in the cracks and do not mind being stepped on occasionally will ensure a harmonious transition from flowerbed to lawn. You should be able to mow over the slabs with your lawnmower without problems.

Stepping stone paths leading through rockeries ensure that you can really enjoy scents and colours. These paths are also useful when work has to be done in the middle of the rockery.

Connecting paths, for example to sitting areas or other parts of the garden, will do their job just as well if they are slightly curved. Bends around mounds of earth or hedges create a walk full of little surprises.

Sunken paths can be used to divide up a sloping area of the garden most effectively (see p. 25).

Short portions of steps forming parts of paths are recommended for sloping areas, as sloping paths may become dangerously slippery on wet days or in the winter.

Steps made of natural stone with gentian, spurge and saxifrage.

Building paths

Regularly paved paths require a lot of preparation and effort so only the building of irregular natural stone paths will be described here. However, all rockery paths will require some preparation.

● Choose stones that are as flat and regular as possible, and will be easy to lay. You will also need to make sure that they are firm for treading on and stable.

● Mark the course of the prospective path with wooden pegs and try out laying the stones.

● Remember to consider the width of the path. Plants should not be allowed to grow all over the path and thus make it unusable.

Depending on the height of the

stones, dig out soil to a depth of 20-40 cm (8-16 in). When set in place later on, the stones should be almost level with the soil so that there is no risk of tripping.

● Tramp down the soil firmly inside this trench and then insert a layer of course gravel or pebbles. This layer should also be trodden down well.

● Lay the stones you have chosen in a bed of sand. The cracks can be filled with soil. Again, tap it all down firmly.

● Now you can plant crevice plants along the edges of the path where they will soon create greenery along the cracks and even over the stones themselves.

Steps

● Natural stone steps should be prepared with a layer of gravel in the same way as paths. The type of stone you use will determine the type of construction you create.

● A simple formula can be used to determine the width and height of the steps: the step height x 2, plus the width of the step, should be 63-65 cm (25-26 in) which corresponds to an average adult stride length. Therefore, if the height of the step is 15 cm (6 in), the width of the step should be 33-35 cm (13-14 in).

Planting along steps and paths

Greenery that can be stepped on: Unfortunately, there are not many plants that do not object to being trampled. Luckily, however, those species that can cope with this then reward us with wonderful scents. Roman chamomile (*Chamaemelum nobile* "Plena"), thyme species (*Thymus serphyllum*, *T. doerfleri*, *T. citrodorus*), *Cotula potentilliana*, *C. squalida*; and on moist, shady paths, blue bugle (*Ajuga genevensis*) and creeping Jenny (*Lysimachia numularia*) will not take amiss the occasional kick or lawn mowing.

Blue and yellow garlands along steps: Lady's mantle, *Campanula portenschlagiana*, *C. poscharskyana*.

Glowing colours, red and white: crane's bill (*Geranium sanguineum*, *G. sanguineum* "Album"). This set of steps will flower all summer long.

Landscaping a slope

In the case of very steep slopes, a natural design (see natural slope, p. 36) will be less suitable. A landscaped slope can be divided up with several low drystone walls in terrace-like steps (see pp. 24 and 38). You will thus create level areas between the small stone walls, which can be used in very

different ways. If the terraced areas are not too wide, the entire slope can be designed as a rockery.

You can plan in paths along broader areas and could even have a vegetable garden or tall bedding plants and roses. Even a sitting area is possible on such a terrace. Drystone walls planted with fragrant thyme can become pleasant garden seats. Steps and paths running through such a setting will offer further possibilites for interesting design (see p. 42).

Cushion plants that turn drystone walls into flowering gems can be obtained for all times of the year.

● Spring – aubrieta, alyssum, phlox, white rock cress.

● Early summer – rockery pinks, mountain avens (*Dryas octopetala*), *Campanula carpatica*, *Eriophyllum lanatum*, thrift.

● Autumn – moss campion (*Silene*), evening primrose, *Sedum cauticulum*, pearly everlasting (*Anaphalis*).

● Winter – houseleek, evergreen *Sedum* species, pearly everlasting, grasses, perennial candytuft (*Iberis*), other evergreen rockery plants.

A multitude of ideas

Water in a rockery

Even the smallest sources of water will increase your opportunities for design. A miniature pond or small birdbath will improve the micro-climate considerably and also benefit the plants as they will require more humidity in a sunny position.
Planting example: A birdbath in the sun or semi-shade. A stone with a hollow in it, or a frost-proof dish let into the ground, are both suitable as a birdbath. Plants can be kept to shades of blue, yellow and white: gentian species (*Gentiana acaulis, G. lagodechiana*), lady's mantle (*Alchemilla mollis*), edelweiss, primrose species (*Primula acaulis, P. veris, P. auricula*), avens (*Geum bulgaricum*), *Campanula portenschlagiana,* saxifrage (*Saxifraga arendsii*), *Deschampsia.*
Evergreen rockery plants and the decorative seedheads of edelweiss, lady's mantle and grasses will also provide decoration in the winter.

Ponds and streams

Small pools or ponds are easy to integrate into a rockery. They should resemble natural mountain lakes or ponds. Suitable rockery plants have been marked with **m** in the table (see pp. 18/19). Four other species can be planted beside the edge of a pond and will also go well with a rockery pool: marsh marigold (*Caltha palustris*), marsh forget-me-not, butterbur (*Petasitis albus*) and *Veronica.* These species will grow in full sunlight or semi-shade.
For skilful do-it-yourself builders, installing a stream will present a special challenge. Naturally, any such installation should be suited to the type of garden you have. Rockery plants that like moist soil and high humidity are easy to combine with plants that grow along the edges of water or on the banks of streams. Water gardens are a specialist subject. If you wish to construct a stream or create a water garden, you should consult an expert landscape gardener or obtain a book that will give you guidance on how to go about this.

A scented rockery

Lovers of culinary herbs can have a field day when designing a decorative rockery. This need not always resemble the traditional, spiral herb bed. A drystone wall that supports a vegetable garden, or a rockery herb bed very close to the kitchen door are both practical and also very attractive. A bed of scented leaves and flowers makes an attractive feature beside a sitting area on a patio. You also have the added bonus of extremely pleasant scents wafting over you.

In addition to lavender and many thyme species, a variety of edible plants can be grown in rockeries. All of them prefer a sunny position.
● Savory (*Satureja montana*) has lilac flowers in late summer.
● Oregano (*Origanum vulgare*) has lilac or pink flowers in late summer and early autumn. The flowers are magnets for butterflies.
● Cotton lavender (*Santolina chamaecyparissus*) has yellow flowers in the summer.
● Salad burnet *Sanguisorba minor* has pink flowers in early summer. Regular cutting will encourage leaf formation in this evergreen rockery plant.
● Sage (*Salvia officinalis*) has blue flowers in summer.
● Chives (*Allium schoenoprasum*) produce lilac flowers in spring. This very decorative plant should not be planted in rows but distributed in small groups.
● *Sedum reflexum* has yellow flowers in spring. It is very suitable for drystone walls.
● *Ruta graveolens* has yellow flowers in spring.
● Hyssop (*Hyssopus officinalis*) produces blue flowers in summer.
● Lemon balm (*Melissa officinalis*) has lilac flowers in summer.
Lemon balm seeds itself and should therefore be cut back immediately after flowering. Lavender, hyssop, cotton

A small waterfall improves the mini-climate and creates a tranquil spot.

lavender, *Ruta graveolens* and sage can serve the function of leader plants in a rockery. They look good on the top of a drystone wall. Low-growing species, like thyme, savory and oregano, should be grouped around leader plants and can also grow in the cracks of walls. Carpet forming thyme species and *Sedum reflexum* will fill out the area and will also grow over stones. Salad burnet and chives are best planted at the foot of the wall. Remaining gaps can be filled with annual or biennial herbs like basil, chervil, parsley, borage, nasturtium or marigolds whose flowers provide edible decoration. Scented violets, cowslips and daisies give spring decoration that is also edible.

Successful care

A rockery will need less attention if the requirements of the plants as to position are considered but you will not be able to manage entirely without some care. Important tips on watering, fertilizing and the prevention of disease and pests can be found on the following pages.

Above: Pasque flowers come in many different colours.
Left: Rock rose looks colourful between the rosettes of Sedum.

Successful care

Care of rockery plants

Rockery plants are divided into three groups.

Bedding plants include many well-known border plants and such splendid herbaceous plants as delphiniums, irises and peonies, which have been raised over many years.

These plants require soil with few other plants in it, plenty of room around their roots and a regular supply of nutrients and water. Some of these species can be used as solitary plants in rockeries. If you take their care requirements into consideration, they can be used to create a varied design.

Pure species rockery plants are plants that have not been interfered with through cultivating or hybridizing. If such plants come from a similar climatic background, you can use them quite easily in your garden. Species rockery plants that have been chosen with an eye to their biological requirements will grow into thick carpet over the years. Regular hoeing or digging would be damaging rather than helpful. Any additional supply of nutrients or water is hardly necessary as long as site-appropriate plants are chosen.

Species plants with bedding plant characteristics form a transition between cultivated bedding plants and species plants. They are usually herbaceous plants that flower abundantly or species that have not been interfered with too much through cultivation, such as astilbe. These plants can be treated like proper rockery plants with respect to care. Their continuous flowering should be ensured through occasional feeding with garden compost.

Plantings that resemble nature

In a very natural rockery you will be able to use mainly pure species of true rockery plants. If you choose the plants skilfully and put together plant communities, such a planting will become ever easier to care for over the years. The rockery plants will grow together to form harmonious plant groupings. Soon the soil will be entirely covered in plants. Few weeds can survive in such an environment.

An occasional careful intervention by the gardener – for example, cutting off deadheads or cutting back very vigorously growing ground-cover plants – will not create much work. A thorough clear up in autumn is not recommended as you would then lose the attractive winter aspect of your rockery.

Care during the first few years after planting

The secret of an easy-to-care-for planting is good preparation of the bed (see p. 22).

Inadequately removed rooting weeds may spoil your rockery forever so, during the first few years after planting, you should keep a keen eye open for signs of weeds. Fast-growing annual weeds or vigorously growing seedlings from wind-blown seeds will prove robust competitors for your delicate, slow-growing rockery plants. Slugs, snails and other pests find excellent living conditions in clumps of weeds, which will also compete with your rockery plants for light, water and nutrients.

Removing weeds: Clumps of dandelions or thistle seedlings are easy to get rid of in the early stages. Once the roots have attained a certain depth, however, they can become a constant plague, especially in loamy soils.

Dense carpets of chickweed, for example, can make life difficult for young rockery plants. Regular, careful hoeing should allow you to remove most of such weeds in their early stages. A blunt garden knife can be used to dig out deeper weed roots. In later years, the hoe should be used less and less.

My tip: A garden knife and secateurs are my most useful and most used garden tools in

The many species of houseleek (Sempervivum) are extremely undemanding if grown in a sunny position.

rockery plantings. The trick is to do the work that is necessary but leave no sign of your interference, such as broken stems or bare patches.

If you have a large rockery with a stepping-stone path running through it, do try to use the stepping-stones and not just balance precariously on any rock that is near your foot. This will cause rocks and large stones to move in the soil and will break or damage foliage and stems. Try to keep children and dogs off your rockery, no matter how much fun it is to clamber about on it.

A houseleek flower.

Successful care

A mini rockery set in the middle of a flourishing garden.

Water and nutrients

Both water and nutrients are necessary for plants to grow and thrive.

● True species rockery plants require water and added nutrients only occasionally if the soil has been prepared properly.

● Larger plantings that have been designed to look more varied and which contain herbaceoous plants, species rockery plants with bedding plant characteristics or actual bedding plants should be supplied in a selective way with additional water and nutrients.

Watering

Making sure that you plants rockery plants in the most appropriate sites is the best way to ensure ease of care later on. Rockery plants that can cope with dry conditions and much sunlight in nature will not require additional watering in similar positions in the garden. Plants that prefer more moisture in the soil should be placed in shady, moist spots in the garden. Plant cushions or stones can function as water storage units just as they would in their natural habitats.

Purposely created hollows and indentations on top of drystone walls create similar opportunities for storing water.

Sometimes, however, additional watering will be necessary, for one reason or another.

To improve humidity: You can increase the humidity in your rockery through occasionally spraying with water in the evening. Mountain plants will supplement your water reservoir by catching any heavy dews that fall at higher elevations. Small basins or containers of water will also help ensure a better mini-climate.

For older rockery plants: Large old plants with voluminous rootstocks that often go very deep are particularly at risk from drying out in very hot summers. Thorough penetrating watering will lengthen their life expectancy and an abundant second flowering will reward you for your efforts. Herbaceous plants and bedding plants in·rockeries are also very grateful for a thorough watering during very dry periods.

Preparation for winter: Evergreen rockery plants should be thoroughly watered before winter begins. This will help them to survive dry periods of frost without snow.

Fertilizing

Good preparation of the soil before you plant will ensure the best possible nutrient supplies in your rockery (see p. 22). During the course of the years, however, the plants will absorb nutrients from the soil and these will have to be replenished occasionally. Well-rotted garden compost is best for this purpose.

● Woody plants, bedding plants and pure rockery species with bedding plant characteristics require regular fertilizing. Small amounts of mineral fertilizers are also recommended, particularly for long- and vigorously flowering varieties.

● Species rockery plants, on the other hand, can manage on smaller quantities of nutrients, especially species grown in sunny, dry positions and heathland gardens. Large amounts of nutrients will lead to massive growth and are quite often the cause of plants dying off. Here, only occasional doses of compost, perhaps mixed with sand, are recommended.

● Rockery plants that originate from the edges of woodland and which you can grow in a shady rockery are grateful for larger amounts of garden compost. The best time to distribute compost between the rockery plants is in the spring. If the beds arc completely grown over, push the compost underneath plant cushions or strew amounts of

well-broken-up compost around the cushions and mats. For plants that like lime, add a little lime to the compost. For heathland gardens and plants that prefer an acid soil, adding a little peat or coarse conifer needle compost is advantageous. Bark compost can be used equally well. Bark mulch is less suitable for rockery plantations. The tannic acid that seeps from unrotted bark can damage delicate rockery plant roots.

It is also possible to use manure to fertilize older drystone wall plants.

My tip: You can prepare your own organic dung solution from cattle manure. A large handful of cattle manure should be dissolved in 10 litres (17½ pints) water. Stir the solution well and let it stand for a few days. Pour the dung solution directly on to the roots of the plants through a spade cleft in the soil during the spring.

NB: A second fertilizing should not be undertaken until the second year after planting at the earliest. Cease to give nutrients by the summer so that woody shoots can mature properly before the beginning of winter. Soft, immature foliage is particularly at risk from frost.

Successful care

Pruning rockery plants

There are three different types of pruning.

The removal of dead flowers: Deadheads should be regularly removed among species that flower for a long time and produce flowers continuously. This will result in a noticeably longer flowering time as the plant is prevented from forming seed and encouraged to keep on producing more flowers. This measure of care is recommended for the following species: avens (*Geum*), red valerian (*Centranthus*), *Inula*, evening primrose, thrift.

Complete cutting back after flowering: This will also encourage a long flowering time or a vigorous second flowering in the autumn. Cut off all deadheads but leave all branches and twigs on the plant. The following plants can be encouraged to flower again by cutting them back: campanula, pinks, rock rose, cat mint, self-heal.

Cutting back dead parts of the plants: Do not remove dead parts of plants until the spring as they form the best natural winter protection. Also, if you are too thorough in tidying up the rockery in the autumn, you will deprive yourself of the enchanting patterns formed by frost and snow on the plants during the winter. In the spring, the work is much easier anyway

as completely dried up plant parts are easily removed by hand.

Rejuvenating rockery plants

Many rockery plants cease to flower so abundantly after a few years; some species even change in appearance. There are several ways of rejuvenating favourite plants.

Using compost: In the spring or autumn, spread well-rotted, finely shredded garden compost directly on or around the roots of the plants. The rockery plants will form new roots and shoots at these points and will be encouraged to produce new growth.

This method can be successfully employed for the following species: coral flower (*Heucherella tiarelloides*), avens (*Geum*), astilbe, phlox, leopard's bane (*Doronicum orientale*).

Division: Remove the entire plant, with its rootstock, from the soil. Depending on the flowering time of the particular species, this should be in the spring or the autumn, preferably on a dull, damp day. Using a sharp spade, or your hand if the rootstock is very loose, divide the rootstock into several fist-sized clumps. Fill up the old planting hole with compost and good garden soil to freshen it up. Plant one part of the plant there again. The other

parts can be used elsewhere.

Propagating from cuttings or by layering downward-hanging shoots: Some rockery plants, like lavender or rock rose, and cushion rockery plants will prove difficult to divide if they are growing in drystone walls. In this case you can try taking cuttings or layering shoots.

● Cuttings will root very well in small pots under transparent plastic hoods on a warm windowsill.

● For layering, choose a long downward-hanging shoot, bury it in soil and weigh it down with a stone. You will know when it has formed new roots by the new growth. You will then have a new plant.

Sowing: Some rockery plants seed themselves; for example, alyssum, aubrieta, valerian, *Corydalis*, cat mint, pinks, Christmas rose, self-heal. It is possible to propagate lavender, edelweiss and carline thistle seeds under transparent polythene on a windowsill.

Winter protection

With good planning and if grown in the right position, rockery plants should cope very well with the winter in a temperate climate. Special measures for winter protection in rockeries and on drystone walls are only essential during the first few years after planting and in elevated regions

Lavender, cotton lavender and sage add their scent to this garden.

with extreme weather conditions. More dangerous than ordinary frosts are frosts without snow (as often happens in a temperate climate), winter sunshine and wet winters.

Good drainage will protect the plants from waterlogging in winter (see p. 22). A protective covering of snow can be simulated in exposed positions with a light covering of conifer brushwood. Parts of plants that have died back are also an effective aid (see p. 52). Thorough watering in the autumn will protect rockery plants and evergreen plants from drying out in winter sunshine.

Spurge laurel in winter.

Successful care

When plants do not thrive

Healthy, vigorous plants will rarely become ill and pests should not be able to harm them greatly. None the less, you should make a daily check on your plants to be sure to catch the first symptoms of disease at an early stage. The following factors are known to favour infestation by pests and diseases:

● unsuitable soil;
● insufficient nutrients or insufficient water;
● unfavourable weather conditions (excessive heat or dryness).

Even newly bought plants may become sickly because a change of position places great strain on a plant. Transplanting favours the proliferation of pests and the infestation by disease.

Diseases

Mildew is the most common fungal disease occurring in a rockery. The symptom of mildew is a white, flour-like film on leaves and shoot tips. Even in dry summers transmission from one plant to another is possible. Mildew can be combated with natural sprays such as mare's tail brew or knotweed extract. Mare's tail brew is most effective if sprayed in sunny weather. As mildew and other fungal diseases generally appear towards the end of the summer, damage is usually not very extensive. Chemical fungicides should only be used for very severe infestation.

My tip: Start in spring with a preventive treatment of mare's tail brew or knotweed extract.

Pests

Aphids: Green or black aphids are found in large quantities on fresh shoots and leaf tips. The leaves curl up and wither. The aphids excrete a sticky juice (honeydew) that attracts ants, bees and wasps. Through them comes the danger of the transmission of viral diseases. Check susceptible plants regularly. Remove the aphids with your fingers or spray the plants with a vigorous stream of water. Spraying with a soft soap solution is the most effective control and kindest to useful garden insects. Agents containing pyrethrum should only be used for severe infestation. N.B. These are not harmful to bees.

My tip: Aphids find it difficult to multiply in plantings containing many different species.

Turnip flies: These small, green, shiny insects jump when touched. They bite holes in the leaves and damage the flowerbuds, which then will not open properly. Mass proliferation is a danger in very dry summers. As turnip flies prefer dry soil, a mulching layer may help. Use tansy tea or brew as a preventive spray. Repeated use of soft soap solution will also help.

Miridae: These 5-10 mm (¼-½ in) long, greenish insects give off an unpleasant odour when touched. They cause crippled shoot tips and leaves. Pick them off by hand.

Slugs and snails: Damage on young rockery plants indicates that slugs and snails are at work. They will also eat flowers. The most effective action is to go on a slug and snail hunt in the dark, equipped with a torch! Beer traps only work with small slugs. Sawdust strewn around sensitive plants will help in dry conditions. I leave it to you to decide how to dispose of them. It definitely does not make sense to throw them over the garden fence on to a piece of waste ground as during the course of a single night the same slugs and snails can be right back in your garden again.

Warning: Do not use slug pellets! In the long run your garden soil will become toxic due to an accumulation of the substance contained in them. Useful creatures that eat slugs and snails, like hedgehogs, moles, birds and toads, will die after consuming poisoned slugs and snails. This will permanently upset the ecological balance of your garden.

Voles, field-mice, moles: The presence of these small mammals can be identified from the appearance of small holes, small mounds of soil and withering plants. Bulbous plants, as well as young, slow-growing herbaceous plants, are endangered.

Plant bulbous plants in wire baskets; a drainage layer of gravel or pebbles will keep moles away; mice can be caught in humane traps.

NB: Moles do not eat plants. All they do is tunnel and push up the soil but they may become pests for that reason. It is said that planting *Euphorbia* will keep moles away.

Try to avoid simply killing wild creatures that come to live in your garden. If they are making a real nuisance of themselves you can try various deterrents or even humane traps. These catch the creatures alive and unhurt and you can then release them far away in the wild. If you have a real problem, ask for advice at your garden centre or nearest wild animal rescue centre.

The five most common pests and diseases

Mildew
Symptoms: Flour-like, white film on leaves and shoot tips.
Occurrence: Often on asters, primroses and speedwell species.
Remedy: Spray with mare's tail brew or knotweed extract.

Aphids
Green or black aphids.
Symptoms: Crinkled leaves.
Occurrence: Particularly on alyssum, red valerian and speedwell.
Remedy: Strip them off with your fingers; spray with a soft soap solution.

Turnip flies
Small, green, shiny insects.
Symptoms: Leaves full of holes and withering flowerbuds. *Occurrence:* Particularly on alyssum, evening primrose. *Remedy:* Spray with tansy tea and soft soap solution.

Miridae
5-10 mm (¼-½ in) long insects.
Symptoms: Crippled shoot tips and leaves. *Occurrence:* On large-leafed rockery plants. *Remedy:* Collecting by hand.

Slugs/snails
Symptoms: Damage through eating of leaves and flowers.
Occurrence: On all young plants, particularly hosta and *Campanula* species. *Remedy:* Collecting the creatures, best done at night.

Successful care

Care all year round

Provided you consider the requirements of individual rockery plants when choosing the planting position, you will not have very much trouble in caring for your rockery.

A few tasks should, however, be undertaken at the right times.

Early spring

Weed control: Lightly hoe around new plants. Carefully remove all weeds.
Nutrient supply: From the second year onwards, spread garden compost on the surface of the soil; depending on requirements, add lime, peat, conifer needles or mineral fertilizer (for bedding plants or herbaceous plants).
Pruning: Remove dead parts of rockery plants.
Rejuvenating: Divide rockery plants that flower in the autumn. This is the right time for adding compost.
Winter protection: Once the frosts are over, remove winter protection.

Mid spring

Weed control: Regularly remove weeds.
Nutrient supply: If you have not already done so, now add compost and fertilizer depending on the plants' requirements.
Winter protection: Keep it at hand in case of late frosts.

Late spring and early summer

Weed control: Regularly remove weeds.
Nutrient supply: Doses of compost and additional mineral fertilizing still possible.
Water supply: If dryness continues, lightly spray in the evenings; water plentifully older rockery plants, woody plants and bedding plants.
Pruning: Remove deadheads; cut back some spring-flowering plants.
Rejuvenating: Rockery plants that flower in the spring can now be divided; add humus; propagation from cuttings and downward-hanging shoots.

Mid to late summer

Weed control: Regularly remove weeds.
Water supply: Lightly spray over in the evening during long periods of dryness; thoroughly water older plants, woody plants and bedding plants.
Pruning: Remove deadheads.
Nutrient supply: Cease to fertilize at the end of summer.
Rejuvenating: Divide plants that flower in the spring and summer in favourable weather conditions.

Early to mid autumn

Water supply: Thoroughly water evergreen and older rockery plants.
Nutrient supply: Compost can be given in the form of mulching layers (winter protection).
Rejuvenating: Divide spring and summer-flowering plants; propagate from cuttings and downward-hanging shoots.

Late autumn

Winter protection: Prepare a supply of brushwood or similar for covering; do not cover until just before severe frosts.

Early winter

Water supply: Water evergreen plants on frost-free days.
Winter protection: Prepare brushwood or similar for protection if you have not already done so.

Mid and late winter

Water supply: Water evergreen plants on frost-free days.
Winter protection: Check during strong wind and gales.

This garden is filled with a summery abundance of flowers.

Index

Author's notes

This volume deals with the design and care of rockeries. Some of the plants described here are toxic. Toxic plants have been marked in the tables on pages 14 and 18 with a warning symbol. Please make absolutely sure that children and domestic pets do not eat plants marked with this symbol.

Take safety precautions when working with very large stones or rocks; make sure that stones cannot slide down a slope and endanger other people. Partially bury the stones in the soil to prevent them from tipping or sliding. When using plant protection agents, keep strictly to the instructions on the packaging. Store plant protection agents and fertilizers (even organic ones) in such a way that they are inaccessible to children and domestic pets. Their consumption could cause illness. These agents should not be allowed to come into contact with your eyes. If you sustain open wounds or other injuries when working with soil, you should consult a doctor about the possibility of a tetanus vaccination.

Cover photographs

Front cover: *Blue spruce - mixed alpines and dwarf conifers, bergenia - pink flowers, Alpine phlox, sabina juniper berberis behind with bronze foliage, varieties of Aeonium and Sempervivum.*
Inside front cover: *Steps made of natural stone give easy access to various parts of the rockery.*
Back cover: *Succulents flowering in profusion on top of stone wall.*

Photographic acknowledgements

Cover photography by G.L. Strong.
Borstell: back cover top left;
msg/Stork: p. 2;
Morell: p. 3 left, 3 right, 16 left, 17 top right, 33 right, 49 bottom;
Nickig: p. 5 right, 10 top, 10 bottom, 12 right, 13 top left, 13 top right, 13 centre right, 16 right, 17 top left, 17 bottom left, 17 centre right, 17 bottom right, 21 right, 23, 26, 45, 47 right, 50, 55 top, 55 bottom, 57, 64/inside front cover;
Reinhard: p. 4/5, 7, 12 left, 13 bottom left, 20/21, 35, 40, 42, 49 top;
Reinhard, N.: p. 13 bottom right;
Schneiders: inside front cover, p. 1, 32/33;
Tipho: p. 37

Reprinted 1998.

This edition published 1997 by Merehurst Limited
Ferry House, 51-57 Lacy Road, Putney, London SW15 1PR

© 1996 Gräfe und Unzer GmbH, Munich

ISBN 1 85391 680 3

English text copyright © Merehurst Limited 1997
Translated by Astrid Mick
Edited by Lesley Young
Design and typesetting by Paul Cooper Design
Printed in Hong Kong by Wing King Tong

A dense carpet of plants

Many rockery plants form dense carpets that may completely cover the soil or a wall. Some use rhizomes with roots to colonize new positions, others lie loosely on the soil like cushions. Among these cushion-forming plants are many attractive flowering plants like alyssum, perennial candytuft or aubrieta. Many species that form rosettes, like stonecrop or houseleek, look attractive even during the periods when they have no flowers. Fleshy or downy leaves are not only decorative but will also protect plants from lack of water or intense sunlight.

Houseleek and sedum show their flowers amid several shades of green.